HANDEL

Solomon

an oratorio for 4 sopranos, alto, tenor &
2 bass soli chorus & orchestra

*the piano accompaniment revised from that
of the German Handel Society*

Order No: NOV 070147

NOVELLO PUBLISHING LIMITED

PREFACE

THE oratorio of *Solomon* was composed by Handel in 1748, the year after he had produced his *Joshua* and *Alexander Balus*. According to the autograph score, preserved in the Royal Musical Library at Buckingham Palace, the composition of the work occupied Handel a little more than a month. He began it on May 5, 1748, and the memorandum at the end of the manuscript is "G. F. Handel, Juin 13, 1748, ætatis 63. Völlig geendiget."

The words of the oratorio are supposed to be by Dr. Morell, but this is not certain. In a few instances the original words have been altered.

Solomon was produced at Covent Garden Theatre, on Friday, March 17, 1749 "with a Concerto," under Handel's direction. The oratorio was revived by Sir George Smart at Exeter Hall, April 14, 1836, and by the Sacred Harmonic Society, December 3, 1838. Costa's additional accompaniments were used at the Sacred Harmonic Society's performance after he became conductor.

The present abridged edition contains only those numbers of the oratorio that are usually performed, the selection being the same as that used by the late Sacred Harmonic Society, and at most of the provincial Festivals.

LONDON, 1897

PART I.

OVERTURE.

8

* *Allegro.* ♪ = 138.

* This movement may be omitted.

DOUBLE CHORUS.—"YOUR HARPS AND CYMBALS SOUND."

13

* The bars between the asterisks may be omitted.

Handel's "Solomon."—Novello, Ewer and Co.'s Octavo Edition.

for ev-er last, will for ev-er last, whose jus-tice, whose truth will for ev-er

pp

last, ... will for ev - - - - - -

- - er, will for ev - er last.

colla parte. *mf*

Praise ye the Lord for all . . His mer - cies, for all, . . .

p

. . . . for all His mer - cies past,

mf

for ev - er last, praise ye the Lord for all His mer - cies

past, whose truth, whose jus-tice will for ev - er last, will for ev - er last,

whose truth, whose jus-tice will for ev - - er last.

DOUBLE CHORUS.—"WITH PIOUS HEART."

-liev'd Thy slave dis-tress'd, With splen-dour cloth'd me,

and with know-ledge bless'd, with splen-dour cloth'd me, and with knowledge bless'd;

Thy fin-ish'd tem-ple

with Thy pre-sence grace, And shed Thy heaven-ly glo-ries o'er the place.

Handel's "Solomon."—Novello, Ewer and Co.'s Octavo Edition.

No. 6.

RECITATIVE.—"IMPERIAL SOLOMON."

Im - pe - rial So - lo - mon, thy prayers are heard.

RECITATIVE (*Accompanied*).—"SEE FROM THE OPENING SKIES."

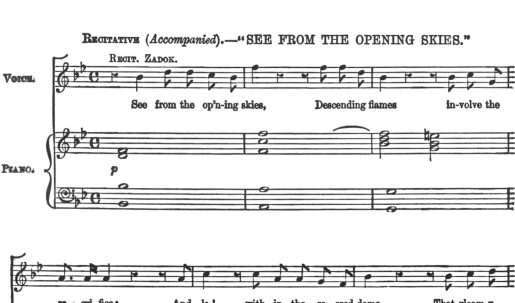

See from the op'n-ing skies, Descending flames in-volve the

sa - cri- fice; And lo! with - in the sa - cred dome, That gleam-y

light, Pro-fuse - ly bright, De-clares the Lord of Hosts is come.

Air.—"Sacred Raptures Cheer My Breast."

Joys . . . too fierce to be express'd, too fierce to be express'd,

In this swell - ing heart I feel, in this swell - - - - - -

- ing

heart I feel;

Sa - cred rap - tures cheer . . my breast; Rush - ing tides of

In this swell - ing heart, in this swell - ing heart I feel.

Adagio.

a tempo.

Warm . . . . en-thu-si-as-tic fires

* The rest of this Air may be omitted.

Handel's " Solomon."—Novello. Ewer and Co.'s Octavo Edition.

In my pant-ing bo - som roll, in my pant-ing bo - som roll;

Hope of bliss, that ne'er ex - pires, Dawns up - on my

rav - ish'd soul, hope of bliss that ne'er ex - pires, . . .

. . . . that ne'er . . ex-pires,

Adagio. *a tempo.*

dawns up - on my rav - ish'd soul. Sa - cred rap - tures cheer my breast;

Adagio. *a tempo.*

fp

DOUBLE CHORUS.—" THROUGHOUT THE LAND."

SOLOMON. (ALTO.)

VOICE.

PIANO.

Blest be the Lord, Who look'd with gra - cious eyes.

Up - on His vas - sal's hum-ble sa - cri - fice ; And has, with an ap - prov-ing

smile, My work o'er - paid, and graced the pile.

No. 10. AIR.—"WHAT THOUGH I TRACE EACH HERB AND FLOWER."

Larghetto.

PIANO.
♩ = 88.

mf

SOLOMON.

What though I

trace each herb and flow'r That drinks the morn-ing dew; Did

I not own Je-ho-vah's pow'r, How vain were all I knew, how vain, how

vain were all I knew, how vain, how vain were all I knew?

What though I trace each herb and

flow'r That drinks the morn-ing dew Did I not

own Je - ho - vah's pow'r,   How vain were all I knew,   how

vain were all   I knew,   how vain,   how vain, how   vain were all   I knew,

how vain were all   I   knew!

Say, what's the rest but emp - ty boast, The pedant's i - dle claim, the

p

pedant's i - dle claim, Who, hav-ing all the substance lost, At-tempts to grasp a name, the

pedant's i - dle claim, the pe-dant's i - dle claim, who hav-ing all the

substance lost, attempts to grasp a name, at-tempts to grasp . . a name.

* The rest of this Air may be omitted.

Handel's "Solomon."—Novello, Ewer and Co.'s Octavo Edition.

And see, my Queen, my wedded love, You soon my ten-derness shall prove; A pa-lace shall e-rect its head, Of ce-dar built, with gold be-spread; Me-thinks the work is now be-gun, The axe re-sounds on Le-ban-on.

O Monarch! with each vir-tue bless'd, The bright-est star that gilds the east; No joy I know beneath the sun, But what's compris'd in So-lo-mon.

Nos. 12 to 19 omitted.

No. 20.   AIR.—"WITH THEE TH' UNSHELTER'D MOOR I'D TREAD.

With thee th' un-shel-ter'd moor I'd . . tread, Nor once of fate com - plain, Tho' burn - ing suns flash'd round my . . head, And cleav'd the bar - ren plain. Thy love - ly form a - lone I

prize, 'tis .. thou that canst im-part con-tin - ual

plea - sure to my eyes, and glad - ness to my heart,

con - tin - ual plea - sure to my eyes, and

glad - ness to .. my· heart.

No. 21.   RECIT.—"SEARCH ROUND THE WORLD."

ZADOK (TENOR).

Search round the world, there ne-ver yet was seen   so wise a monarch,   or so chaste a queen.

1st SOPRANO.

sleep with their song,

2nd SOPRANO.

sleep with their song,

sleep with their song,

Ye

sleep with their song,

Ye

sleep with their song,

Ye

while

ze - phyrs, soft breath - ing, their slum - bers prolong, while night-in - gales lull them to

ze - phyrs, soft breath - ing, their slum - bers prolong,

ze - phyrs, soft breath - ing, their slum - bers prolong,

night-in - gales lull them . to sleep with their song, while night-in-gales lull them to

while night-in gales lull them, while night-in-gales lull them to

sleep, to sleep, to sleep with their song, while night-in - gales lull . . them to

while night-in - gales lull them to

while night-in - gales lull them to

sleep with their song,

sleep with their song,

sleep with their song, Ye

sleep with their song, Ye

sleep with their song, Ye

while nightin - gales lull . . them to

while nightin - gales lull . . them to

while nightin - gales lull them to

while nightin - gales lull . . them to

while nightin - gales lull them to

sleep, ... to . . sleep with their song.

sleep, ... to sleep with their song.

sleep, ... to sleep with their song.

sleep, ... to . . sleep with their song.

sleep, ... to sleep with their song.

p

pp   *ritard.*

END OF THE FIRST PART

Handel's "Solomon."—Novello. Ewer and Co.'s Octavo Edition.

PART II.

No. 28. DOUBLE CHORUS.—"FROM THE CENSER CURLING RISE."

Handel's "Solomon."—Novello, Ewer and Co.'s Octavo Edition.

No. 28.   RECITATIVE.—"MY SOV'REIGN LIEGE."

Handel's "Solomon."—Novello, Ewer and Co.'s Octavo Edition.

Bore my soft dar-ling from my arms a - way, And left her child be - hind, a lump of life-less

clay ; And now, oh impious! dares to claim My right a-lone— a mother's name.

No. 29. AIR AND TRIO.—"WORDS ARE WEAK TO PAINT MY FEARS."

VOICE.

A tempo giusto.

PIANO.

A tempo giusto.

f

FIRST WOMAN. (SOPRANO.)

Words are weak to paint my

p

fears; Heart-felt an-guish, start-ing tears, Best shall plead a mo-ther's cause; Words are

weak to paint my fears; Heart - felt an-guish, start - ing

tears, Best shall plead a mo-ther's cause. To thy

throne, O King, I bend, to thy throne, O King, I bend, My cause is just, be thou my

friend, my cause is just, be thou my friend, be thou my friend, my cause is just, my cause is

just, be thou my friend!

SECOND WOMAN. (SOPRANO.)

False is all her melting tale, false is all her melting tale, false is

all her melt-ing tale, false is all her melt-ing tale, false is all her melt - ing

tale,

My cause is

SOLOMON. (ALTO.)

Then be just, and fear the laws,

Jus - tice holds the lift - ed scale, ... Jus - tice

just, be thou my friend! To thy throne, O King, I .. bend,

False is all, false is all her melt-ing

holds the lift - ed scale,

My cause is just, be thou my

tale, false is all her melt-ing tale, Then be just, and fear the laws,

Jus - tice holds the lift - ed scale, ...

friend, my cause is just, to thy throne, O King, I

false is all her melt-ing tale, false is all,

. . . . Jus - tice holds the lift - ed

bend, My cause is just, be thou my friend,

Fear the laws, false is all her melting tale, Then be just, and fear the

scale, Jus - tice holds the lift - ed

my cause is just, be thou my friend, my cause is just, be thou my

laws, fear the laws, false is all her melting

scale, the lift - ed scale, ...

friend ! Words are weak to paint my fears; Heart- felt

tale,

Jus - tice holds the lift - ed scale,

pp

an-guish, start-ing tears, Best shall plead a .. mo - ther's cause.

false is all her melting

To thy throne, O King, I bend, My cause is just, be thou my

tale, false is all her melting tale, then be just and fear the laws.

Jus - tice holds the lift - ed

friend, my cause is just, be

scale, .. Jus - tice holds the lift - ed scale.

Handel's "Solomon."—Novello, Ewer and Co.'s Octavo Edition.

thou my friend, be thou my friend, my cause is

just, be thou my friend.

Each claims a - like, let both their portions share ; Di-vide the babe ; thus each her part shall bear ;

Quick, bring the falchion, and the in-fant smite, Nor fur-ther cla-mour for dis- pu - ted right.

No. 81. Air.—"THY SENTENCE, GREAT KING."

VOICE.

Allegro.

PIANO.

Allegro. sempre.

f

SECOND WOMAN. (SOPRANO.)

Thy sentence, great King, Is

p

prudent and wise, thy sentence, great King, is prudent and wise; And my hopes on the wing Quick

bound for the prize, my hopes . . . on the wing quick bound, . . . quick

bound for the prize;

thy sentence, great King, is prudent and wise, is prudent and wise,

my hopes . . . . . on the wing quick bound for the prize, quick

Handel's "Solomon."—Novello, Ewer and Co.'s Octavo Edition.

bound for the prize, my hopes on the wing quick bound for the prize, my hopes . . .

. . . on the wing quick bound, . . . quick bound for the prize.

Con - tent - ed I hear, And ap - prove the de-cree, con - tent-ed I hear, con -

- tent - ed I hear, and ap - prove the de - cree, For at least I shall tear . . The lov'd

in-fant from thee, for at least,   for at least   I shall tear,   I shall tear,   at least, the lov'd

in- fant from thee, the lov'd in - fant from thee, for at least   I shall tear   from   thee,   the lov'd

in -fant from thee ;   Con - tent- ed I hear and ap -

- prove the de-cree, and ap-prove the de-cree,   For at   least   I shall tear The lov'd

in - fant from thee,   for at   least   I   shall   tear   the lov'd in - fant from thee.

No. 32. RECITATIVE.—"WITHHOLD THE EXECUTING HAND."

FIRST WOMAN. (SOPRANO.)

Withhold, withhold the ex-e-cu-ting hand! Reverse, O King, thy stern command!

No. 33. AIR.—"CAN I SEE MY INFANT GORED."

Largo ma non Adagio.

FIRST WOMAN. (SOPRANO.)

Can I see my in-fant gored With the fierce re-lent-less

sword? Can I see, can I see, can I

see him yield his breath, Smi-ling at the hand of death? can I see him,

can I see him? And be-hold the pur-ple tides Gush-ing

down his ten-der sides, and be-hold the pur-ple tides gush-ing

down his ten-der sides? can I see? Ra-ther be my hopes be-

- guil'd; Take him all, take him all, ra-ther be my

hopes be-guil'd, take him all, but spare my child!

No. 35 omitted.

so wise as So - lomon? Who, who, who like Is-rael's king is . .

so wise as So - lomon? Who, who, who like Is-rael's king is . .

so wise as So - lomon? Who, who, who like Is-rael's king is

so wise as So - lomon? Who, who, who like Is-rael's king is

wise, so wise as So - lomon? Who, who, who like Is-rael's king is

f   *mp*

blest, who like Is-rael's king is . . blest? Who so wor - - - -

blest, who like Is-rael's king is . . blest? Who so wor - - - -

blest, who like Is-rael's king is blest? Who so wor - thy of a

blest, who like Is-rael's king is blest? Who so wor - -

blest, who like Is-rael's king is blest? Who so wor - thy of a

f   *cres.*

No. 37.   REGIT.—"FROM MORN TO EVE."

ZADOK. (TENOR.)

From morn to eve   I could enraptur'd sing   The various virtues   of our happy King;

In whom, with wonder,   we behold combin'd   The grace of feature   with the worth of mind.

No. 38.   AIR.—"SEE THE TALL PALM."

Allegro moderato.

ZADOK.

See   the tall palm, that   lifts   its   head,

see the tall palm, that lifts its head On Jordan's sedg-y side, on Jordan's sedg-y

side, Its tow'r - ing

branch- es curl - ing spread, its tow'r - ing branch - es curl - ing

spread, ... And

bloom . . in grace - ful pride.

colla voce. *f*

And bloom .. in grace - ful pride, See, see the tall palm, that lifts its head, Its tow'r - ing branch- es curl - - ing spread, ... And bloom in grace ful pride.

Nos. 39 and 40 omitted.

Handel's " Solomon."—Novello, Ewer and Co.'s Octavo Edition.

* The original time-signature of this Chorus was $\frac{6}{4}$. The eight bars forming the Introductory Symphony have been taken from bars 47 to 54 of the accompaniment.

(119.)

PART III.

SINFONIA.

No. 42.

man - sion, fit for kings to own, The fo - rest call'd of tow'r-ing Le - ba-non, Where

Art her ut - most skill dis - plays, And ev' - ry ob - ject claims your praise.

No. 44.   AIR.—"EV'RY SIGHT THESE EYES BEHOLD."

Allegro moderato.

VOICE.

PIANO.

NICAULE, QUEEN OF SHEBA. (SOPRANO.)

Ev'-ry sight these eyes be - hold   Does a

Handel's "Solomon."—Novello, Ewer and Co.'s Octavo Edition.

That my soul does most de - light, that my soul does most de -

- light, ...

that my soul does most de - light, that my soul does

Adagio.

most de - light; Ev - 'ry sight these eyes be - hold

a tempo.

Does a diff'- rent charm un - fold; But to

hear fair truth dis - till - ing, In ex - pres - sions choice and thrill - ing, From that tongue so soft and kill - ing, That my soul does most de - light,

that my soul does most de - light, . . .

. . . . that my soul does most de - light,

But to hear fair truth dis - till - ing From that tongue so soft and kill - ing, That my

No. 45.   RECIT.—"SWEEP THE STRING."

Sweep, sweep the string, to soothe the royal fair, And rouse each passion with th'alternate air.

Handel's "Solomon."—Novello, Ewer and Co.'s Octavo Edition.

DOUBLE CHORUS.—"SHAKE THE DOME."

No. 48.

REOIT.—"THEN, AT ONCE, FROM RAGE REMOVE."

No. 49.

CHORUS.—"DRAW THE TEAR FROM HOPELESS LOVE.'

tear from hope-less love, from hope - less love; Lengthen out the so-lemn air,

hope - less love, from hope - less love; Lengthen out the so-lemn air,

hope - less love, from hope - less love; Lengthen out the so-lemn air,

. . the tear from hope - less, hope - less love; Lengthen out the so-lemn air,

hope - less love, draw the tear from hope-less love; Lengthen out the so-lemn air,

Full of death and wild des - pair, full of death and wild des -

Full of death and wild des - pair, full of death and wild des -

Full of death and wild des - pair, full of death and wild des -

Full of death and wild des - pair, full of death and wild des -

Full of death and wild des - pair, full of death and wild des -

Handel's "Solomon."—Novello, Ewer and Co.'s Octavo Edition.

No. 50. RECIT.—"NEXT THE TORTUR'D SOUL RELEASE."

SOLOMON. (ALTO.)

Next the tor- tur'd soul re - lease, And the mind re - store to peace.

No. 51. AIR AND CHORUS.—"THUS ROLLING SURGES RISE."

Allegro moderato.

SOLOMON.

Thus roll - ing sur - ges rise, And plough the trou- bled main; But soon the tem - pest dies, And all is calm a - gain, and all is calm, but soon the tem- pest

Handel's "Solomon."—Novello, Ewer and Co.'s Octavo Edition.

Nos. 52 and 53 omitted.

RECIT.—"THRICE HAPPY KING."

ZADOK. (TENOR.)

Thrice hap-py king! to have a-chiev'd What scarce will henceforth be be-liev'd;

When sev-en times a-round the sphere The sun had led the new-born year,

The Tem-ple rose, to mark the days With end-less themes for fu-ture praise;

Our pi-ous Da-vid wish'd in vain, By this great act to bless his reign; But

Heaven the monarch's hopes with-stood, For ah! his hands were stain'd with blood.

AIR.—"GOLDEN COLUMNS FAIR AND BRIGHT."

ZADOK. (TENOR.)

Gold - en co - lumns, fair and bright, Catch the mor - tal's ra - vish'd sight, . .

Round their sides am-bi-tious twine Ten-drils of the clasp - ing vine;

Che - rubim stand there dis-play'd, O'er the ark their wings are laid; Ev'- ry

ob-ject swells with state, ev' - ry ob-ject swells with state, All is

pi - ous, all is pi - ous, all is pi - ous, all is great, . . .

all is pi-ous, all . . is great,

twine   Ten-drils of the clasping vine;   Che - ru-bim stand there dis

- play'd,   O'er the ark their wings are laid, Ev' - - ry

ob - ject swells with state, ev' - - ry ob - ject swells .. with

state, All, . . . all is pi - ous, all, .. all is pi - ous,

all is pi - ous, all . . . is great,   ev' - ry

ob-ject swells with state, ev' - - ry ob-ject swells with state,

Adagio.

all is pi - - ous, all . . is great.

Adagio.

No. 56. Double Chorus.—"PRAISE THE LORD WITH HARP AND TONGUE."

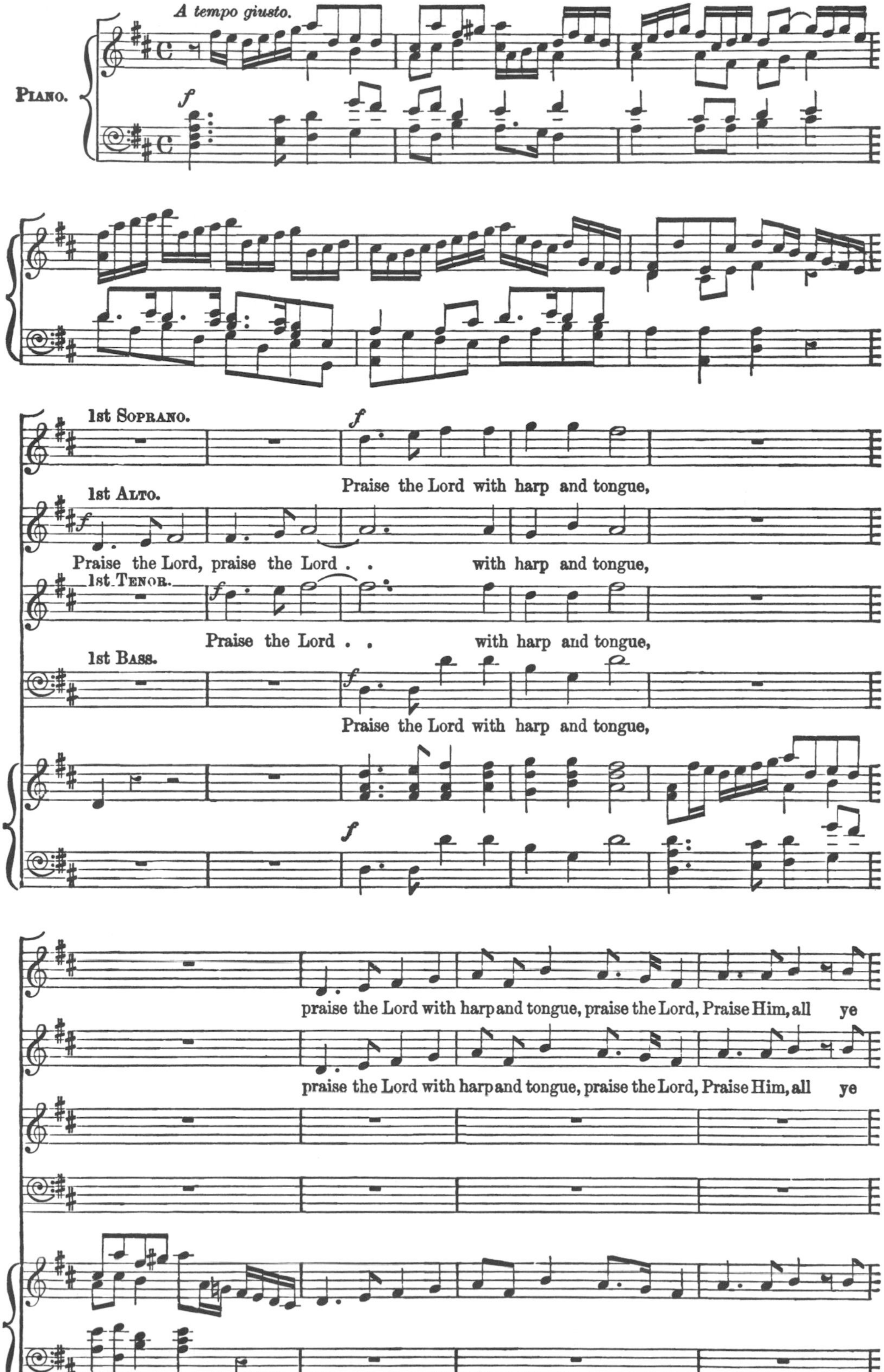

No. 61.
RECIT.—"ADIEU, FAIR QUEEN."

Adieu, fair queen, and in thy breast May peace and virtue ev - er rest.

No. 62.
DUET.—"EV'RY JOY THAT WISDOM KNOWS."

Larghetto, con moto.

Ev' - ry joy that wis-dom knows, May'st thou, pi-ous monarch, share, may'st thou, pi - ous monarch, share, Ev' - ry joy, ev' - ry joy that wis - dom knows, May'st thou, pi - ous monarch, share;

SOLOMON.

Ev' - ry bless-ing heav'n be-stows, Be thy portion, be thy portion,

virtuous fair, virtuous fair, virtuous fair, Ev' - ry bless-ing heav'n be-stows,

Be thy por-tion, vir-tuous fair.

Gent-ly flow the roll - ing days,

Sor-row be a stran-ger here;

Praise unbought by price or fear, May thy peo-ple sound thy praise, Praise unbought by

Praise unbought by price or fear, Praise, . . . Praise unbought by

price or fear, praise unbought, praise unbought, praise unbought by price or fear,

price or fear, praise unbought, praise unbought, praise unbought by price or fear,

May thy peo-ple sound thy praise, Praise unbought by price or fear.

May thy peo-ple sound thy praise, Praise unbought by price or fear.

Printed and bound in Great Britain by
Caligraving Limited Thetford Norfolk

1 2 3 4 5 6 7 8 9

INDEX.

PART I.